earth

Technically Earth, Air, Fire and Water are not considered
elements in modern science. The Greeks included these
four as "elements" in their science because they believed
them to be the four basic qualities which made up all
substances.

Translation: W. Brian Altano

Pedagogical text: Cecilia Hernández de Lorenzo

First English language edition published 1985 by
Barron's Educational Series, Inc.

© Parramón Ediciones, S.A.
First Edition, September 1984
The title of the Spanish edition is *la tierra*.

All inquiries should be addressed to:
Barron's Educational Series, Inc.
113 Crossways Park Drive
Woodbury, New York 11797

Library of Congress Catalog Card No. 85-6086

ISBN 0-8120-5742-2 (hardcover)
ISBN 0-8120-3596-8 (pbk.)

78   987654

Printed in Spain by Sirven Grafic, S.A.
Gran Vía, 754 - 08013 Barcelona
Legal Deposit: B-43.046-86

the four elements
earth

Carme Solé Vendrell

J. M. Parramón

CHILDRENS PRESS CHOICE
A Barron's title selected for educational distribution

ISBN 0-516-08692-8

Imagine...imagine...

An immense space

where it sometimes rains,

and when it rains, plants, flowers, and trees grow

and rivers and seas are born,

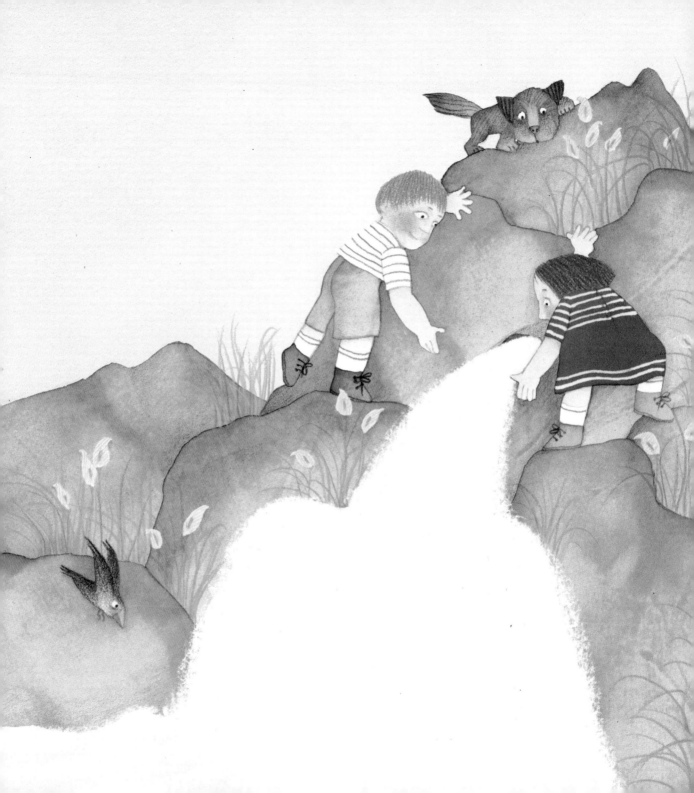

...where the fish live...

...and all the animals!

Imagine a marvelous place...

...where there are fields, woods, houses, cities...

...mountains, caves, stones, rocks...

...iron, coal, silver, and gold...

...a place where we all live. Can you imagine it?

IT'S THE EARTH!

EARTH

All life develops in the earth, that of plants and that of animals depend on the life developed in the ground.

The ground we walk on

It surrounds us on all sides. It's not smooth nor continuous. Mountains, valleys, rivers, seas form a spherical surface full of irregularities.

The soil comes from the changes in the rocks that make up the earth's crust.

The rocks that form the earth

Rocks are not all equal. Pick up two rocks the same size and compare their weight. Do they float on water? A few, like pumice, do.

Granite is a hard rock. It was formed inside the earth, at high temperatures, ascending in the form of *magma* and becoming hard in the subsoil, before coming to the surface. It is an *igneous* rock.

Limestone is a *sedimentary* rock. It was formed at the bottom of the sea from the sediment carried by rivers. If you look at it carefully, you will see the remains of marine fossils.

Slate is a relatively hard rock that has the property of breaking into smooth and thin sheets. It is a *metamorphic* rock that comes from the transformation undergone by igneous or sedimentary rocks when submitted to conditions of high pressure or temperature.

To compare the hardness of rocks, try to scratch one against the other. The harder rock will scratch the softer one.

Erosion, separation, and decomposition of rocks by water, wind, or sharp changes of temperature have caused the appearance of different types of soil.

Look at the ground

Take a handful of dirt and break it up with your fingers. It is composed of a mixture of sand, silt, clay, and humus in greater or lesser proportions, according to the specimen.

In deserts and beaches, the principal component is sand. With wet sand you can build a castle that will crumble little by little as it dries out. Sandy soil does not retain much water, and it is poor earth for cultivation.

If the soil is *clayey* (composed chiefly of clay) you can shape it and bake it and you'll get pieces of ceramic. This soil is formed by very small particles that are sticky when they get wet. Clayey soil is difficult to cultivate, but very fertile. You can recognize it because when it dries it cracks and when it's wet it's almost impenetrable.

Limy soil is good for cultivation. This soil is very fertile, sticky when it's wet, dusty when it's dry, very soluble and porous. Under limy soil you can find caverns and underground streams.

The soil in a broadleaf forest is *humic,* dark, full of dried leaves, tree stumps, and animal remains, all those particles with the power to retain water. It is very fertile.

Do you see something else in the specimen?

Who lives in the ground?

In a handful of earth you can find worms, insects, bacteria, fungus.... Some of these organisms contribute with their displacement to aerate the soil, making it more porous and permeable. Others catch the nitrogen in the air, enriching the soil with nitrogenous compounds. Others decompose the organic substances that are the soil, producing humus.

Furthermore, the ground serves as a support for the roots of plants. Numerous animals live on it, and the buildings where people live rise up from it.

The treasures the ground hides

In addition to learning to cultivate the earth, we have learned to take out its treasures.

As early as the Stone Age, people searched for *flint* to make fire and stone for tools. Later, they learned to mine bronze and iron; then coal, oil, and natural gas; and today uranium, a source of energy in nuclear power plants. And we shouldn't forget the most precious treasures of all time: diamonds, gold, silver....

Our earth

The earth is something more than just the ground we walk on. It is our neighborhood, our city, our culture, our language, our friend, and the inheritance we will leave to our children.

Let's urge all the people who live on it to cooperate to make it better, to make ourselves better. Let's direct our efforts to eradicate the hunger, sickness, and misery that is still suffered today in many places on our planet.

It is people who belong to the earth and not vice versa. By respecting and loving nature, people respect themselves, and their future existence depends on this.